Praise for *Red Silk* by Maryfrances Wagner

I have admired the work of Maryfrances Wagner for ̶ ̶ ̶ ̶wenty years as have legions of her students and readers. Now ̶ ̶ ̶ *Red Silk* is cause for our celebration, for here are the ̶ ̶ ̶ ̶ ̶ ̶ ̶anged as both a personal memoir and a cul̶ ̶ ̶ ̶ ̶ ̶ ̶ ̶ ̶ ̶ecades. Each section of this powerful boo̶ ̶ ̶ ̶ ̶ ̶ ̶ ̶ ̶ ̶ue—from the ravages of the Vietnam War, ̶ ̶ ̶ ̶ ̶ ̶ ̶ ̶ ̶ ̶u marriages and national integrity, to the poet's battle ̶ ̶ ̶ ̶ ̶ ̶ ̶ ̶ ̶ner loving acceptances of middle age in middle America. An̶ ̶ ̶ ̶ ̶ ̶ ̶ ̶out the poems waves the figure of red silk. Is it a bloodied bandage? A piece of lover's clothing? A flag? A teacher's corrective? It is all of these and more. If her poems are plainspoken, woven into tight lines, Wagner's book accumulates into an inclusive, sympathetic document of post-nuclear American life, as delicate and as fiery as red silk itself. In the end, Maryfrances Wagner knows the hardest knowledge: that the personal is the political, as the erotic is the elegiac.
—David Baker, *Kenyon Review*

"I can almost touch what he feels," Maryfrances Wagner writes in her last poem, "Depth Finder," and although she is writing of her husband who is staring out the window at the lake, "listening to the wind's/breath and his own become one," the words also apply to the reader engaged by the compelling poems of *Red Silk.* Her gift, abundantly apparent in these poems, is to draw the reader into her poems especially through her meticulously crafted images. All of Wagner's poetic gifts are brought into play in the Vietnam poems: taut and sharp-edged language, resonant imagery, concision, drama, emotional intensity. Wagner's triumph in the end is that after reading the poems you might touch the cover of her book and imagine that you are touching red silk.
—Brian Daldorph, *Words Is a Powerful Thing*

Not only does Maryfrances Wagner's tight, detailed imagery, use of sound, and keen perceptions in Red Silk lead readers through four decades of U.S. history, it carries them through songs of innocence and experience from a female's point-of-view. The initial section opens with a shy, young girl's persona and follows her through "First Days" of school, where she "flushes" because she must repeat the pronunciation of her Italian last name, its "four vowels clogging the tongue" for her teacher, who stumbles with it. By the second section, the girl has become an adult who shares classroom experiences from a teacher's point-of-view, including when she drives past the grade of a one student she lost when a car ran over her, and later, when she sits at the "Front of the Bus," where her students "won't see the thinning spot" in her hair. With its symbolism of passion and sacrifice. "Red Silk," its "dye breaking ties," opens the third section, comprising letters from her fiancé fighting the Viet Cong, their marriage, and its demise. And the final section displays a powerful, positive vision, but with a caveat in its last poem, "Depth Finder." One of Wagner's best, it warns lovers how we must sometimes hold back—monitor our emotions, lest we feel too much and lose it all, our hearts bleeding into a profusion of red silk.

BkMk Press, one of the nation's top literary presses, has re-released this award-winning collection by Missouri's new poet laureate, mainly because its language, rhythms, images, and themes remain as vital today as they were when it came out in 1999. It's well worth re-reading—a second—and even third—time.
—Lindsey Martin-Bowen
Where Water Meets the Rock, Crossing Kansas with Jim Morrison

Red Silk takes readers on a profound journey from a title poem full of pain and tragedy to the final poem aptly called "Depth Finder" in which little happens but what matters most. The most moving poems here will not date. They are more than politically acute or fashionably adept. They deal with the human concerns that go beyond the rise or fall of markets. Maryfrances Wagner's poems have the texture of actuality, the courage of candor, that sense of life that is not just poetic. Who cares what this poetry is labeled; it gets under your skin.
—Dan Jaffe, *Round for One Voice*

The poems in this work are precision word choices that capture the fear in love and the love in fear and the lives that continue to evolve as they daily move through the massive personal experience of living. There are no accusations in these poems. They allow the reader to share lives evolving in turmoil, lives full of the daily activity of growing and becoming, of lives touching so softly the moments of joy in the midst of anger and violence. These poems capture the atrocities of war and challenge of living when it might simply be easier to die. They provide basic recognition of the joy present in eating and drinking while capturing massive puzzles within self-destruction. These poems are personal but universal. Maryfrances Wagner has taken *Red Silk* and metaphorically transferred the image as a symbol for accessing the joy of living while sustaining a belief in self.
—David Anstaett, Scattering Skies Press

RED SILK

Also by Maryfrances Wagner

The Silence of Red Glass
The Immigrants' New Camera
Light Subtracts Itself
Salvatore's Daughter
Tonight Cicadas Sing
Bandaged Watermelons and Other Rusty Ducks
Pouf
Dioramas

RED SILK

POEMS

Maryfrances Wagner

BkMk Press
Kansas City, Missouri

Originally published by the Mid-America Press
Reprinted by BkMk Press 2022
www.bkmkpress.org

BkMk Press titles are distributed to the trade
by the University of Arkansas Press.

Cover design: Greg Field

ISBN 978-1-943491-34-6

With thanks to Greg Field, my husband, soul mate and writing partner. His valuable advice and high standards always drive me on. Thanks also to the fine critical eye of Robert Stewart who sometimes helps me see differently. Thanks to those who have supported, offered advice or cheered me on: Robert C. Jones, David Anstaett, Dan Jaffe, Gay Dust, Janette Williams, Sheryl Shreve, Sonya Stokes, and Judy Roberts. Finally, thanks to Gale E. Wagner who gave me permission to publish parts of his letters with his blessings.

༄

What we call the beginning is often the end
And to make an end is to make a beginning.
The end is where we start from. . .

And any action

Is a step to the block, to the fire, down the sea's
throat
Or to an illegible stone: and that is where we start.

—T. S. Eliot
Little Gidding

Illusions mistaken for truth are the pavement under
our feet ....

—Barbara Kingsolver
The Poisonwood Bible

ACKNOWLEDGMENTS

The following poems were published in present or previous versions in the following:

Any Key Press Zine ("The Immigrants Get a New Camera," "Final Impressions"), *Avenues into Another Millennium: A Missouri Anthology* ("Scimeca's," "Sorting Things Out"), *Birmingham Poetry Review* ("Victims Lose Direction"), *Coal City Review* ("Homing"), *Laurel Review* "The Results of Some Hoping"), *Potpourri* ("Softening Up," "Depth Finder"), *Thorny Locust* ("Long-Distance Love," "When the Pollen Count Is Up"), *Unsettling America: An Anthology of Contemporary Multicultural Poetry* ("Miss Clement's Second Grade"), *Voices of Italian Americana* ("Gardenias").

CONTENTS

1

2

3

4

RED SILK

1

Even the seasons form a great circle in their changing and always come back again to where they were. The life of a [person] is a circle from childhood to childhood.

—Black Elk

NEW STARTS

Uncle Phil says he doesn't cover
them anymore, shows me
his fig trees, grown from starts
my father gave him years ago.
Eight years, I tell him,
since I've eaten a fig plucked warm
from trees that reached over our heads.
A special gift, my father said
when he packaged figs in baskets.
I couldn't imagine it then, the figs
weighty and full, abundant at meals.
My uncle's trees are short, like bushes.
They die back when winter comes.
He's potted two cuttings for me,
one the blue, one the white mission fig.
He advises mulch and manure.
*You don't have to cover them
as your father did.* I recall wrapping
mummies against Missouri snows.
With a hand that looks like my father's,
Uncle Phil plucks for me
one of his seven figs,
a touchstone to summers
of limitless figs, oozing their
honeyed gleam on trays,
always enough for gorging and giving,
enough for the file of ants lured by
nectar. *Taste it,* my uncle says.
Small but sweet, it's a private
communion of mixed blessings.

3

4

Maybe my uncle knows the weight
of this gift as he lifts his eyebrows
and raises his hand in a gesture
I know well. We carry my starts
to the car, the taste of fig on my tongue.

THE IMMIGRANTS GET A NEW CAMERA

No one knew when they stood on Stanley Hill,
each waiting to hold the new family camera.
They didn't mind sharing among the eleven of them,
one capturing the bridge over the north end, another
the city skyline, the old airport. Sadie took candids
of Josie scratching her bites, Lena hiking up her
sagging skirt. Sam lined up Gene and Phil saluting,
Jay making a pig face, Nene showing his new tooth
coming in, all of them in costumes they'd found
at the dump. It was all about holding the black box
for the first time, framing those frozen moments
before listening for the lever's click. Frank snapped
Rosie singing "The Continental" while she swished
the yellow skirt of her dance hall costume,
little Martha imitating her sister's swing,
Nene turning somersaults down the hill.
No one knew they couldn't afford film.

FIRST DAYS

Slumped over in my back-row chair,
I sat every September, twisting my
ring around a moist finger, rolling
new pencils on my desk to air out
my hands, waiting, always waiting,
that pebble hardening in my throat.
Pat Adams, Billy Brown, easy names.
Only I made the teacher stumble,
four vowels clogging the tongue.
As the teacher waited, I repronounced
my name, my voice a wobbly pushcart
squeaking down the aisle, my hands
creeping up my face to cover a flush.
By Diane White and Dennis Yates,
I could swallow again.
After roll sheets and the inky scent
of new books lured me to Pharaohs,
pronouns or pie graphs, my feet
shuffled under my desk,
trying to find their place.

MISS CLEMENT'S SECOND GRADE

They sat in even rows
like new chocolates in a long box,
quiet enough to hear pencils
trying uneven letters.

On those days Maria stared
at clean blue-lined paper
while boiler heat sifted
through thumping registers
by Anthony's desk.

Maria shaped vowels,
and wished she were a Smith
so she could hand out crayons,
have her papers on display.

During quiet writing,
when everyone seemed the same,
she almost forgot
the hours locked in the teacher's closet.

Every day Miss Clement wore a navy dress,
tied her blond hair in a circular braid.

Every night Maria laughed
with Wilbur and Charlotte.
They didn't mind her Italian name.

THE TURNING OF WHEELS

If there is any ultimate stuff of the universe, it is pure
energy . . . . the dancer and the dance are one.
—Dancing Wu Li Masters

Two blocks from home, Beverly waved,
shouted for me to join her across the four-lane
boulevard. It was forbidden to cross. I shook
my head, but Elizabeth Taylor paper dolls
and cinnamon fire sticks overpowered the warning
in my head. I inched off the curb.
Three lanes of cars stopped to let me cross.
I ran hard, my eyes on Beverly, her checked dress,
her knees bowed above her brown saddle shoes.
In the fourth lane darkness swallowed me,
spit me through a tunnel into a shower
of light, a particle in space.
I hovered above drivers peering over
the motionless body. An ambulance wove
between the clog of cars. Paramedics
pushed a stretcher as Beverly's lunch box
flashed around the comer. I floated,
a buoyant dot, a seed gliding in an updraft.
Her heels clicking on pavement, open
coat flapping, arms waving like a flag,
my mother hurtled down the street,
begging the medics to wait. She wobbled
into the ambulance on a broken heel,
stumbled to her knees and squeezed my arm.
I tumbled through space and gasped.
I could smell her lipstick, feel her pulse,
the wool of her coat brushing my arm.
I reached for my head, where pain shot
in every direction. The soft, fluid heat

with its iron smell matted my hair,
crusted in my hands. My head lolled
as my mother cupped my shoulder.
My eyelids rolled shut with the turning
of wheels, the siren's whine slipping away.

EASTER CHICKS

My brother brought them home from Lou's Drug,
where he unpacked boxes, a dozen pink and blue
chicks, peeping and thumping beaks inside
their cardboard box. As Anthony argued
to keep them, I named the orphans,
merry-go-rounded them on the turntable.
Except the two that walked between porch balusters,
ten chicks grew feathers and roosted on the porch,
outgrowing cages my father hammered and screened.
When the rooster started crowing before dawn,
Mrs. Pardington pulled her robe sash tighter,
shook a fist at our porch. My mother
crossed her arms, peering out at free-ranging
Harry pecking paint blisters, said time they went
to Uncle Newton's farm to eat crickets, feel grass
under their feet. I could spend the weekend
with cousin Phyllis when she took them.
On Saturday, Phyllis and I straddled
crabapple limbs, pictured Harry leading
the girls around, Uncle Newton hooking bass.
On Sunday, my mother had fresh-squeezed lemonade
waiting, my grandparents already sipping theirs.
As my father sliced bread, Mother set
a steaming bowl of rice on the table.
Where's the pasta? I asked.
I needed to cook these, she beamed, but I knew
when she slid one on my plate, it wasn't
the ducks Father shot with Uncle Carl.

MAGIC FEET

When he failed chemistry,
spent grocery money on comic books,
broke his retainer again, she chased
him around the table, her yardstick
a foil plunging after him.
He always joked her into a good laugh,
and she never delivered a blow.
Somehow they ended up dancing,
a tango down the hall, a fox trot in the kitchen.
Sometimes they shoved table against window,
stacked chairs, rolled up the rug, and dragged
out 45s. There on her prized parquets,
waxed too often, buffed every week,
they danced, sock footed, their sidekicks
and twirls digging into that shine.
Her shirtwaist flounced and belled;
their arms waved above their heads.
He swung her over his back,
and she slid into the splits through his legs.
Hip bumpers, foot thumpers,
mother and son rocked until time to put supper on.
Furniture back in place,
report card, comic books, or retainer
waited on the table for dad.

MR. COHICK'S PHYSICAL SCIENCE CLASS

Among thin-necked beakers, Mr. Cohick
perched over his lab table, waving long,
chalky fingers. We groaned at his puns
as he sent electrical charges sizzling
through wires or inspected our petri dishes
blooming germs we'd scraped from bathroom
sinks. To each of us he gave a nickname:
Charley Harley, Makish, Annie Mae.
One afternoon, while we drew cloud
formations, he told us how to figure
exactly when it would rain. As he dug
around under his lab table for his next
demonstration, I crossed my legs
to feel the texture of my silky stockings.
The memory of Eddie Arbor's breath
near my ear crowded my thoughts.
I rolled and unrolled my black turtleneck,
pinched my earlobe and watched shreds
of cirrus clouds inch over the stadium.
So then, what might this be, Cush,
his nickname for me. I fell through
layers of space. He held a long box.
Charley Harley stared. A thin whistle of air
rose from the heater, wavy as my thoughts.
Shrugging, I watched his eyebrows arch
like wooly worms. *You don't know*
what a thermometer is? Leady Eddie
humphed through his nose. Makish rolled
her eyes. I stared at thunderheads
sketched in my notes, felt them gather charge.
I sizzled Mr. Cohick, but I never forgot
how to figure when it would rain.

SCIMECA'S

I still drive across town for Romano,
a fresh chunk I grate at home,
for black and green olives ladled
from crocks, for family-made sausage,
wrapped in butcher paper loaves,
weighed on an old-fashioned scale.
It's a family business, an old grocer and son
caught between frozen pizzas, low-fat dinners
and the old way: fresh ricotta, gallons
of olive oil, bins of rigatoni, penne.
My uncle, two blocks from the grocer,
weighs moving to a condo against staying
near his sister and the community center
where friends talk about the old days.
When I gather homework from my crowded
classroom, I weigh their faces against
former classes of waving hands.
Although sometimes I am the tipped end
on a scale like Mr. Scimeca's son,
I am always weighing toward the balance
of how things are. With new lessons,
I still teach my students, my uncle
stays in the old neighborhood, and I make
my jaunts to Scimeca's so my red sauce
will taste like my grandmother's
as my mother's did.

2

What a devil of a profession! But it has its charms.

—Voltaire

THE RESULTS OF SOME HOPING

Ardith is last down the steps,
the only student lugging books in a fire drill.
Like a bird, she tilts her head at me, same way
her mother, Lydia, did twenty years ago.
Red-headed Lydia sputtered and wheezed
whenever she raised a hand, all of us shifting,
setting down pens, some hoping
she'd raise those eyes above clusters of tissues,
afloat on her desk like wilted gardenias.
I untangled her from hooks and latches,
but wished just once she'd open her locker
on the first try, not call out for me to wait.
Lydia, the only girl unable to run a lap,
dribble a ball, the single pep squad member
waving a crew-sweatered arm
among cheering v-necks, the lone girl
stumbling down bus aisles,
snagging her spiral on jackets.
At the door, Ardith leans
into her sliding geometry book
A pencil and highlighter bounce off her elbow.
We shoo her into open air, scramble for books
fluttering pages behind her.
As she measures the last step with a toe,
her red hair spirals in the wind;
a flurry of Kleenex lifts from her purse like doves.

FINAL IMPRESSIONS

Every morning, I drive past the bent railing
under the willow, the spray paint still vivid,
though the crosses and wreaths are long gone.
Once my students tied laminated poems
on those branches, in memory of Kathy,
one of four students I've lost this way.
The neighbors left them up all winter,
fluttering on yam bows, some mornings
winking like Morse code.

I remember so well the day before,
Kathy reading her poem about Jeff,
her yellow bow bobbing as she shifted
from foot to foot. She sketched for us
the blue dress she'd sewn for prom
and dotted in her grandmother's pearls.

Usually the quiet girl hunched at her desk,
she pulled layers of hair across her face
and bowed her head when I asked for readers.
She pressed so hard when she wrote,
I could feel the puffy braille of her paper,
read impressions left on the under page.

Afterwards, we read elegies, our eyes
drifting to jags of light reflected from her
empty chair. We walked to the funeral
as a class, drawn faces, watching
the shoes in front of us. We stared
at her picture framed on the coffin.
She wore the blue dress, the pearls.

Perhaps it is better to go in a heat
after the slow dance beneath the spinning,
mirrored ball, breath warm on a bare shoulder,
moist hands clenched, a rose corsage wafting
its notes; knowing at last the sweetest juices.
The moment when we press so hard
before the oncoming car spins across the lane.

FLEDGLING

Trimming back the straggling spirea,
I thought of Melissa in sophomore English
telling the class she never had a curfew.
She wrote in her journal about the memory
of her cousin rubbing against her,
skin to skin, in the dark. She watched
Terel shoot Brian in the eye.
It was no accident, she told us, *and he
wasn't sorry either. He lied to get off.*
Clipping twigs into bundles,
I startled two puffs of baby blue jays,
more stomach than wing,
bumping around in the marigolds.
They hopped in the garage,
smacked beaks on concrete.
With my attempts to piper them
near their mother's caw,
they backed into the guttering,
turned to each other and squawked.
I shooed Whiskers back in his own yard,
left the jays to their flying lesson.
By afternoon they'd skimmed
the lawn but never quite lifted.
I hung my clippers, still thinking of Melissa
dropping out to stay with the baby
she brought home from daycare bruised
and scalded. By morning, when I reached
for the paper, two flattened tufts
were smears in the street, a single tail feather,
barely forced, stirred in the wind.

MY SOPHOMORES VIEW THE ECLIPSE

We set aside Brutus's soliloquy
to poke pinholes into paper,
tear a second sheet for viewing.
Today we have permission to watch the eclipse.
Mickey, without permission,
explains the process they've already heard.
Worthy of her role as Casca,
Emily stabs her paper five times
then checks the mirror in her purse
where the eye sees not itself/ But by reflection.
At 11:30 they spill down the steps,
like runners on Lupercal, and scatter
out the door, warning each other not to look up.
They line up their sheets of paper,
see half a moon, half a sun.
Kastavas, who loves honor more,
lifts his face and hands to the sky.
See, nothing happens, he insists,
impervious to wrinkles, words
blurry on a page, numbness in an arm.
These are the years of unquenched
weekend thirst, when t-shirts sport
skeletons or Megadeth, announce *No Fear.*
I watch my students view the sun secondhand,
with only a pinhole of light.
When we shuffle back to Brutus,
they wait for me, who thinks too much,
to explain what the lines really mean.

THE POTENTIAL OF INTENTION

Every April I stare from the window
at my tomato plot, forget about leaf hoppers
and hornworms, the plunder of squirrels,
locked into the memory of Father's perfect
Jet Stars, reddening on sunlit windowsills.
I tum soil to let frost do its work, later
add manure, soil, lime, let the ground
warm. When I nestle in young plants,
new leaves unwind in early rain, dark
and strong on branches. Flowers give
in to strings of green beads. I water deep,
weed, and fertilize, stake sagging green
balls. The first tomato comes early
in July, a Big Girl I hold up to the light.
Then the long wait for another. Rainless
days of Missouri sun brown and wilt
leaves. Sun scald, black fungus,
teeth marks mar my Beauties.
The compost heap steams with wasted fruit.
Beneath new soil, rocky clay gives back nothing.
Some still come to the table firm and juicy.
Even the invaded, if not thick slices,
are team players in salads and stews.
Every April the memory of those meaty
Big Boys drives me onward to turn the plot,
those Celebrities filling canning jars,
spotlighting garlic and olive oil in a marriage
with basil. With more lime, more manure,
this year's crop will escape black spots
and leaf wilt. I dream of baskets full again,
unblemished with blossom end rot.
This year no horn worms will get them
before they bear fruit.

FRONT OF THE BUS

On the bus trip, I sit so my students won't see
the thinning spot I can't cover with tint.
I know it glows like a burning bush
where the sun has fingered its way in.
From the back, laughter trumpets past
snippets of small talk weaving together
on a slow float forward. No one sits,
for the first time, where I can add
connections to this patchwork of teen talk.
Years ago, I sat on a bus behind Ms. Krumsiek,
taskmaster of looming demands.
No one sat near her as she stared past
these same empty trees, heard
the same lumber of bus wheels.
Behind her back, we imitated how she
nodded off during the Hardy book panel,
boasted about prize-winning roses,
pronounced spelling's two *l*'s like a *w*.
Yet we were her proud flock,
perched over our pens, thirsty for white paper
when she cannoned vocabulary in steady fire,
ready to guess a character's epiphany.
Once, delivering a book, I found her
standing among her hundreds of roses,
sunlight haloing her luminous face
as she clipped me a fragrant handful,
tucked one in my thick, brown hair.
For the year I inherited her classroom,
I searched for her handouts, imprints
she left on the blackboard, but found her
only in my voice instructing students.

24

Without a protagonist to lead us,
we each take our seat at the front of the bus.
In the rearview mirror, a stranger stares
back, her face with its own story.

3

. . . honor is a whirlpool, a play of confused forces, an illusory moment in the flux of opinions. It is a sense-deception, as when a swarm of insects at a distance seem to the eye like one body. . .

—Kierkegaard
Purity of Heart

VICTIMS LOSE DIRECTION

In a blizzard, snow surrenders direction,
unsure if it's snow or sleet, one with the wind.
A man once walked through a blizzard to bring me
a yellow rose and a package wrapped just like
a Bicycle-deck queen of hearts.
He was unlike my father, except he knew
how to mend the broken, build what he needed.
Once he built a tetrahedron kite we flew
in an open field of wild flowers. With him
I cracked my first lobster, unsure about forks.
He rescued me from the undertow of a barge
when our canoe tipped on the Missouri River.
He helped me raise six baby rabbits
he recovered from a deserted nest.
He sent dozens of yellow roses.
Through that blizzard, his eyelashes iced,
his jeans crusted, he never lost his way.
That took knee-deep rice paddy mud,
unspearing men from pungi pits,
stepping on a Claymore mine.
After months in Army hospitals,
he folded an origami diamond, identical
to the engagement ring inside. But he couldn't
mend nerve damage, soften welds of scar tissue.
In a blizzard, victims lose direction, see
what isn't there, collide with what is,
become one with the sleet pocking away at them.
The bridesmaids wore daisies in their hair,
the groomsmen dress blues. Guests threw
rose petals as we stepped through a saber arch
supported by wounded vets, our smiles
mirrored over and over on the sharp blades.

28

RED SILK

I
You sent five yards of red silk
woven with white-patterned leaves.
It stretched down the hallway,
a long shimmering train.
I rolled across its soft sheen,
wrapped it in a sari, a sarong,
flapped it until it billowed, then sank
over me, a flutter of moth wings,
and slid down my arms like mercury.
I dreamed it into a kimono, a robe,
before pinning down papery skins
of patterns. A wedding night negligee
would hug curves and pool into yours.

II
As scissors clipped where light glowed
against shadows, a booby trap
exploded. Its hot, broken stars
split you open, rib cage to groin.
Blood arched and runneled
into the jungle's red clay.
The chopper dusted silt into your glistening
wounds. To the hovering soldiers,
you signaled a Churchill V .
The silk pieces slid from my fingers
when the telegram arrived.

III
From hospital windows you watched
acorns fall twice. Surgeons couldn't rewire
the short-circuited nerves in your arm,

mend the double hernia. One testicle,
half a stomach would suffice. The leg
would swell always. On weekends
I couldn't make the flight, I laid
the silk remnant on the pillow,
waiting for your call.

IV

In the third June, I pressed finished
seams, the iron gliding itself, its radiant
glow startling beside the ivory veil.
Your wounds had scarred into stiff
and knobby steel welds. When the negligee
slid across your arm, you felt it
in your fingertips. Scars rubbed against me
hard as a grate.

V

In sudsy water, the negligee
bled in red streams, dye
breaking ties with the silk.
From a hanger, the gown
dripped red puddles on the floor,
drying a pink shadow of itself.

LETTERS FROM VIET NAM

23 Feb 68
Chu Lai

The flight over took twenty hours. Rockets and mortars had
hit the airstrip before we landed in Bien Hoa. In the bus to
Long Binh, chicken wire covered the closed windows to
keep VC from throwing in grenades. We sat in air
conditioning, listening to Nat King Cole sing "Those Lazy
Days of Summer." This place is crazy as hell. I will
fit in here perfectly.

On the morning of the 21st we flew to Chu Lai for a six-day
orientation. Then to Duc Pho thirty miles south. We'll be
fighting the 42nd regiment of NVC and VC—fairly good
terrain, not a lot of fighting, a good place to get started.

I've never seen so much drinking. A quart of Vodka or gin
costs a dollar. My BOQ is on the South China Sea about a
hundred meters from the water. It could be a resort in
Hawaii. Fighter jets go over at least once an hour on
 bombing runs, choppers about every thirty seconds. Inside
we play slot machines, drink beer, listen to music from
Saigon. This is my kind of Army over here.

2 Mar 68
Chu Lai

It's a rainy afternoon. "Love is Blue" was just on the radio.
Damn, it could make a guy homesick. Well, we just
finished our orientation. Three miles away in the
mountains the VC are thick. At night they throw rockets and
mortar to remind us they are there. Jets on bombing
missions fly over while we play hearts or chess, read, write
letters. At night we watch movies. The PX's have
everything from TV's and ice boxes to sex books, canned
fruit, and cigars. This morning I did some shopping for

you. I bought you five yards of red silk. I thought maybe you'd like to make something with it. It's like a city here without flush toilets except everyone carries weapons. A flush toilet would sound as good as the Temptations. Tomorrow we go to the field in Duc Pho. America's best men are here. The morale is high.

11 Mar 68
Duc Pho

I have been platoon leader for five days. Life in general is great. Along with us, the infantry, is a company of engineers and a battalion of 155 howitzers. Our AO is east along the South China Sea and west to the mountains. Charlie sneaks up to the perimeter at night. The Army over here is my way of life.

The first day, I lost one of my men, blown to hell by his own Claymore mine. Static electricity detonated it, but he was careless. I was on top of the hill eating chow when I heard the explosion. I had to pick up his pieces and wrap them in a poncho. For the first time in my life I felt helpless. Though I like it and think I should be here, I can still hate it.

Sometimes when I feel down, it's easy to feel more down. The bunkers are small. We sleep three high, like a jail cell. We have a dirt floor and only a small port hole for firing. The front yard is bare dirt for a hundred meters, so we can see Charlie. Rolls and rolls of strung barbed wire serve as our fence. What did Frost say about "good neighbors"? Trip flares and mines give Charlie a proper welcome.

My RTO makes me lemon pudding every day. His mother sends it from home. My men know I like cigars, so they give me their rations. Roi Tan falcons. Lousy in the states, but they taste great here. It's a nice feeling having a platoon of good men. We all want one thing in common:

to go home alive. Yesterday my RTO was baptized. He had to inspect weapons around security and beat a VC captive to death with his bare hands.

My CO and I went to see *Count Dracula*. While we watched the movie, VC probed the perimeter. One day we shell a village. The next we patch up the wounded who aren't VC. It's a crazy war.

Last night one of my men received word his wife delivered an eight-pound boy. He bought the platoon three cases of beer. A couple of men got so drunk they fought. Another disobeyed an officer. Minor problems.

Try not to worry about me. I actually think I belong here and wouldn't trade the experience for any in the world. I saw a *KC Star* the other day. Sure looked good—even the want ads. I miss Huntley Brinkley. We hear less about the war than you do.

17 Mar 68
Duc Pho

I lie on my wooden rack at night and think about you. I'll be in the field for eight days, so I can't write. Someday again I will relax and sleep at night without waking to bombs and shells. I've smelled what I never want to smell again, but I know I will. I've got twenty klicks ahead of me tomorrow with a full pack. Ask your dad to explain a klick.

25 Mar 68
Duc Pho

I know you want to hear the whole works on Nam, but some things I won't tell you. The TOE strength of a rifle platoon is 43 men. I've been operating with 22. In the last eight days I lost six more men. A scout dog team led us into a booby trap. Everyone was hit except me. All are now in Japan. I lost another man in a pungi pit. They even put footprints on top of the pits. It's no fun to yank a bamboo stick from a man's rear while he's screaming. Another was one of my best men—a really tough Brooklyn street fighter. He got it in the head while we were blowing a bunker. It was his second time hit. Both times bad, both times he walked to the dustoff.

The bullets hit all around us. I want to get down and kiss the dirt, but my job is to see where it's coming from and organize against the enemy. My RTO and I watched the bullets riddle a well a few feet away. The smell of charred bodies is one I won't forget. I've watched men bleed to death. I've watched men torched. It's not what I want to talk about. I'm fine and adapting well. I feel I belong. I've learned to accept the ill taste. We aren't fighting the NVC yet. The VC are sneaky but not as apt to stay and fight like the NVC. Tell me about school.

I always carry an American flag in my pocket. I put the flag up on the radio antenna to harass the VC. I feel like 17 million dollars—no ill effects from malaria pills or c-rations. Don't let human nature get the best of you and worry. If I lived here I'm sure I'd be a VC. It's hard to explain. I've discovered and seen most of what I came to see.

3 Apr 68
Duc Pho

I've gone out about thirty times now. I've killed. I've torched. I've watched men die. I've almost killed people with my bare hands because of what they did to my men. You get versatile or you snap. Today we shot an 18-year old girl five times. The two shots in her back took out the front as they went through. She tried to kill us with a grenade. How nasty it is to watch a wife hug her husband just splattered in a fox hole. She dragged his body into a hole and covered it while his guts left a trail behind. The best part of my day is when I sleep and all is black.

Sometimes I call in artillery so close it scares the men. They plead for me not to but we have to get a hole in their defense to get out before we die. How do I tell the men when we are surrounded that we're almost out of ammo. What can I think when all men around me get hit, but I don't? The leaves fall next to me, and if I'd been inches to the right or left, it would have been my head.

Tomorrow my mission in VC territory will be with thirteen men instead of 43. We'll stumble in the dark on ambush. When Charlie shoots, I can't let the men fire because he'll see the muzzle flash and zero in. The next time I hear the national anthem I know I'll almost cry.

I got a tube of toothpaste off a VC body. I'll keep it to show you. I feel I've aged every day, but I still wouldn't trade the experience. I miss you. Happy Easter.

24 Apr 68
Duc Pho

Hello, hello. I like your smile. Won't you wait a while. The weather must be beautiful back home. My favorite time of the year. All is going well with me. Still feel like twelve million dollars—however that feels.

4 May 68
Duc Pho

We're on a seven-day operation. The pen I'm writing with I took off a VC we killed. You remember Campo, my RTO, the one who made me lemon pudding and drank Kool-aid? He was hit by a booby trap yesterday. It really hurt me. He made his promotion to E-5 that day but was hit before he got the word. Could you write him and send him Kool-aid? His girl married a hippie while he was over here. I can•t find out how badly he was hit. I knew it was in both legs, the right arm, elbow, chest, neck and head. He was directly on top of the booby trap.

The rice paddies are full of mud, sometimes knee deep. Nothing is as tiring as humping through three miles of rice paddies—unless it's humping the mountains with jungle canopy and a full pack. The mud has human and buffalo waste. It sticks and slops and slurps as we wade through. Sometimes the men get stuck. When we cross streams, men get leeches. I've seen them eight inches long. When I pull one off, a man can bleed severely. When Charlie snipes at us, we have no cover, but hedge rows cover the hills. We hack them with machetes. Bamboo thickets line the rivers. Thorns tear at us as we push through. Mosquitoes are everywhere. When we sit, ants overwhelm us. When we eat, flies cover our food, our bodies—at least a hundred if we're lucky—usually more. We sweat, and the flies stay because we can't bathe the stink off.

Maps show villages long destroyed by war. People live in straw houses with dirt floors. In our AO all of the schools and churches have been destroyed. Some of the VC have been women. I've found VC hiding in holes under the river beds. Tunnels are everywhere. It takes a man seeking medals to enter a tunnel. They have several levels of rooms, halls, escape routes. The people become moles. A blast in there will shatter a man's eardrums—if he gets out alive.

The other day we fired on two VC out of M-16 range. We covered the area with machine gun fire then searched it out. The VC were gone, but we had killed a little girl about eight years old. Tell me how you think I felt. It's not easy either to tell a man he'll be fine when I know he'll never walk again. The people here are caught between two stronger forces, trapped with no where to go but into death's mouth. Tell me nice things about home. Tell me about a ball game. I'll never tell you the nasty facts. They're just too unpleasant.

1 May 68
Lz Ryder
19:30

We moved north for awhile. I'm in the big mountains and thick jungle. Insects click. Monkeys chant. My men wonder what I'm like in civilian life and what kind of girl tolerates me. Send me a picture so I can show them. Can't get any word on Campo. Thanks for the tapes. I love all of the songs. I damn near wore the tape out listening to the parts with your voice.

23 May 68
Due Pho
Lz Bronco

While up north someone stole $400.00 from me. It's the cash I'd saved for our R & R. Guess I'll have to get in a few more card games. My tour in the field is half finished unless I decide to extend it. I've become too close to my men and hate to leave them. Last night I pulled a few strings and got them 14 quarts of whiskey. They fight like men but drink like kids. Had to babysit many to keep them from tearing up the place. It's hard to send men out on missions when their wives are expecting a baby the next week or they talk about fishing with their sons or they confront the Dear John letter. Then war becomes personal. Campo is going to be all right They had to butcher him to get all the steel out. No scars on his face, though.

I'm listening to the *Rhapsody in Blue* tape you sent. What an artist. I'm sending a map of one of the areas I worked.

Don't mean to cut you short, but some of my men just came
to donate to my R & R fund.

30 May
Due Pho
Lz Dragon

Back home at dragon. It's been 120 degrees, and we hump
with 70-100 pound packs all day in the jungle. Every day I
dust off men who pass out. This increases our loads
because we still need 2800 rounds of machine gun ammo,
mortar rounds, claymores, personal gear, etc. We start at
5:30 and go until 19:00, sometimes midnight. We set
ambushes at night and still never find Charlie. He knows his
country well. When the CO makes unwise decisions, it's
hard on morale. As much as I hate to admit it, this war is
sapping a lot out of me. A year from now I want to be at the
Indy 500. I haven't drunk enough to feel the effects since
I've been here. Actually, from what I watched, I doubt I ever
shall drink again except .on special occasions.

10 June 68

I'm no longer a platoon leader. About ten days ago I was
hit by a 105 howitzer booby trap. I have had surgery twice
and again tomorrow. From here they're flying me to

Japan. Then back to the states. Ticks me off I didn't get to
finish my tour. This mean no R & R I knew I'd get hit
before I came over. I am okay and should have use of all
major limbs. Even getting the hell knocked out of me has
been a good experience. When I was hit, I lost my last flag.

20 June 68

I still feel like ten million dollars. Can't write much right
now.

26 June
Chu Lai

Haven't been able to move much since the last surgery. I I
can't focus either. In three days I leave for Japan. I'm
going to try to come back to Nam to finish my tour.
Yesterday I walked for the first time. Even though the body
is messed up, the mind affects the condition. I know I'll be
fine. I talked with my doctor for two hours last night about
snakes.

28 June 68

Stitches came out from the initial surgery. Healed up well.
No one will see the scars even with shorts on. No one
except you. Hey, you can never have enough American
flags. When I was hit I lost my favorite pair of boots. I was
going to bring them home. They went through everything.
They looked nasty, but someone cut them off my feet at
dustoff.

1 July 68
Japan

Happy fourth of July. My progress is outstanding. Can
walk now for a while rather than a few feet. Still can't focus
more than ten feet. Today I saw a flush toilet even though
I didn't use it. I called mom and dad. It was so unusual to
dial a telephone again. Let me know when a good time is
to call you. After I left the field, the new platoon leader was
off by 2000 meters. All of my men were hit with booby
traps.

3 July 68
Japan

After talking to you I want to come home. I should be healed around your birthday and ready for my next duty station. I miss my platoon. They were brothers, family. Something seems missing now. When I was doped up in the hospital, my abdominal wounds still open, I tried to walk out and get back to my men. They stopped me and calmed me down. Someone came to draw blood. I thought he was one of my men and we were on the hill. I finally realized he wasn't, but I still thought I was on the hill. I had to find my men, so I belted him. Later we became friends.

I feel my largest achievement was shaping some duds into soldiers. Most of them acted like boys. Most didn't want to be there. One dud took over a month to straighten out, but the day I was hit, he took care of me like a brother. When they put me on the chopper, I raised both my arms, one to make a V as Churchill did, one formed an O for ok. When I had a man injured by a booby trap, I always burned the village to the ground. Still feel like a million dollars. I should be back in the states before long. I miss you.

WOUNDED IN CHU LAI

*Under fragrant bait there is certain
to be a hooked fish.*
                —Sun Tzu

Pieced together in a wobbly scrawl,
letters fragmented like an engine's
stuttering start. They describe
the Quonset Hut lined with faces
like choir boys, holding the open vowel.
You shiver under a sheet,
thinking of your men on the hill,
until the needle finds a vein.
Tubes drip blood and fluids.
The nurse debrides your open wounds,
plucking scabs, dead tissue,
shrapnel from the mine.
Morphined, you rocket
out of yourself, a ribboned pole
topped with a machine-gun nest,
spiraling up into stars. When orderlies
lift you to clean white sheets, a latexed
arm reaches down your throat, peeling you
inside out. At night, the ward
is a litany of moans, the drugged garble
of men sloshing through mud.
The bandaged soldier beside you
collapses into himself; Death
.wrestles out the last glow.
On the ceiling, a platoon of helmeted
shadows march forward, jabbing air
with beyonets, grenade pins locked
between their teeth. The point man,
in crossed bandoleers, whacks

with a machete at your bandaged head,
a piñata filled with jungle dreams. Morning,
doctors check nerve damage. Their faces
melt into your platoon, caught in ambush,
calling your name for orders. "Fire,"
shouting, "Fire!" you rise through the brain's
short circuits, ricochet off walls
where spiders feed on each other,
tapping messages on a master web
that traps every wounded soldier,
hooked on the same line.

WEDDING NIGHT

The downtown skyline swallowed the stars.
On our Hilton balcony, we sipped champagne.
You stared beyond the darkness, strings
of car lights guiding you there. We crawled
between crisp sheets, soon slippery with sweat.
You stared at the ceiling, chewing your nails.
I was a kink in this knot of wounded soldiers,
a phantom limb. Four would go back
to Fitzsimmons for skin grafts, a new arm,
throat surgery, a rebuilt jaw. The rest
would have to return home. I dressed
for the drive back to the recovery ward
in fatigues, huddled around a poker pot,
chugging beer, shuffling green bills,
our apartment filling with stories
I could now recite: Paul's 27 bayonet
wounds, saved by his killer dog;
Whisper ripping out his trachea; Campo
speared in a pungi pit; Company B torching
villages, the children, running flames;
grenades, mortars, Claymores, dustoffs.
Dress blues hung in plastic bags from knobs,
artificial limbs, a heap above empty fifths
rolling into sleeping bags. From Jim Perry's leg,
we drank beer passed around like a long draft.
You scooted up to the table, lifting
that fresh scotch in a toast to them.
I crept into the darkness of our bed,
new sheets singed with cigarette burns,
holding the smell of somebody else.

FIRST MONTH

A white haze settled on counters in the tiny
apartment kitchen when I sifted flour for
muffins, rolled flaky pie dough. I pureed
in the new blender, stirred sauces with herbs,
diced, chopped, deboned with new Cutco knives.
Meals steamed at the table in wedding china,
Hot biscuits puddled coins of butter by your
empty plate, gravies congealed. Three A.M.
caterwaulings hustled me from sleep.
You serenaded the neighbors with Boy Scout
songs while strumming a golf-club guitar, shouted
Army marching drills or slurred how everyone
should come out to see the moon. Ms. Campbell
shook her fist from the window, left taped notes
on our door. I tried to lure you in with leftovers:
stroganoff, t-bones, chicken divan.
Your hair was a smoky bar room
when you lodged your chin in my shoulder,
backed me into the bedroom, unzipped
your fly. No time for the flirt of eyes,
the clasp and nestle of limbs, the sizzle of foggy
kisses once savored on the old airport road
as jets reversed their engines above us.
The moon was a cool white bowl, waiting for me
to whip meringue for a pie. When I reached for it
in the oven, it would be hot and ready
because I'd given it time.

SHADOWS

One afternoon the medals arrived
in satin-lined boxes with a letter
thanking you for service.
After months of surgeries, Fitzsimmons
had stitched all visible wounds,
but staph still squirmed in your scar tissue,
blanks you shot couldn't offer children,
the jungle festered in your head.
You stroked the silk ribbons, palmed
the heft of the metal, then closed
the boxes and tucked them
in your sock drawer. Some nights,
nightmares jarred us both, you
shouting orders, scuttling from bed
to a crouch on the floor. One night,
I found you staring off, watching
clouds unravel across the moon.
Socks pooled beside the chair,
leg swollen again, you massaged
your arm as though it might make
feeling come back there instead.
The room was full with shadows,
the smell of scotch, smoke.
Silver Star, Bronze Star, Purple Hearts
lay on the ottoman beside the letter.

FACES

Like a man drunk on the rage of being alive.
—Yusef Komunyakaa

In the photograph we toast a birthday,
two dozen faces clinking glasses, before
liquor loosened tongues, before you punched
the goose egg on Jeff's eye. Jeff or Joe,
I can't attach names to these grins.
Memory is a red welt. In time, it fades
like this party. I remember punches,
the tangle of fallen legs, soggy carpet.
It took four to drag you into the bathroom.
You pummeled the door until wood split,
yanked towel bars from the wall.
The glass votive you smashed
against the mirror streamed hot wax
on the finger towels, across the tiled floor,
in the spider web of cracks mirroring
the phantasmagoria of faces, your masterpiece
of performance art before the truck driver
rendered you unconscious. I remember
the hard draw of breath, pounding feet
rushing outside, the steady line of Fellini faces
staring from car windows as they floated past
until the street was quiet, except the choking
of my own engine as I loped off into the dark.
I bolted and chained the door, but it
was only a gesture. Like splinters
of streetlight, leaking between curtains,
you would find your way in.
By morning, swollen and split-lipped,
you would deliver familiar promises,
broken by dusk with thirst.

AMBUSH

You returned after three days,
your jacket a sketch of stains,
your face gashed again.
Silhouetted in the doorway,
you rummaged through my purse,
elbowed me away when I lunged
for the strap, and shot out the door.
I trailed in your wake. My lipstick
rolled like a wasted shell. The compact
gleamed a signal in the streetlight.
You sifted through pens, glasses, keys.
What you want is in *Chu Lai,* I screamed.
Billfold pictures arched and fluttered
like clipped wings. I scooped them up,
teeth chattering, *You should have had*
a second tour. We stared at each other,
hope unspooling like the thread that wove
the red silk you sent from Danang.
We were braided green,
now dried in a wreath we couldn't untwist,
couldn't make straight again.
We shuddered in darkness.

SEPARATION

In the quiet of separation, the rooms were mine.
No socks huddled around the chair,
no coffeetable rings, no empty cans.
In this tidy quiet, I roamed, touching what
remained whole, dusting where light filled
empty spaces, not expecting you to check in
singing *For What It's Worth.*
You plucked dats from the board to try
for the bull's eye, asked to borrow my car.
The flatbed had dropped its muffler,
your latest car already in salvage.
Your eye on the target for the last dart,
you swore you wouldn't be drinking.
You suggested a round of Liar's poker,
folding a bill between your fingers.
All evening I stood guard, waiting for the tripflare.
I had lit three candles on the same match.
I was watching the cat lick its paw
when the hospital called. Thanatos
had sent you back again. Three times
the only survivor, thrown through the window
before the fist of fire exploded the car,
chose the trapped woman instead,
the other driver wheezing his last breath.
I scraped the windows of a borrowed car.
Dodging scar tissue, surgeons tied off
black sinew across your face, down your leg.
Sitting up, you delivered your favorite line,
"I feel like ten million dollars."
If every stitch holding you together were a mile,
I could have snorkeled in Key West

or watched Alaskan salmon return like you.
Instead, I shuttled you back with crutches,
your face a map I'd never travel,
to that quiet space neither of us wanted you to go.

GHOST IN STARLIGHT

> *The heart has reasons of its own....*
> —Pascal

Ice clinking like chest medals, you paced
the dark, caught in a space too dense
to pass through, a ghost in starlight.
Your cigarette's coal was a bobbing signal,
indecipherable. I watched from the bedroom,
picking the lock of my own story.
Weeks of street fairs, bead shops, coastal
drives had brought us here to encircled
ground. No party at Peter's would unravel
seams of silence. All those words,
becoming moonstones inside our stomachs,
couldn't ascend to tongues. In that summer
we tried again, your new turf
a thousand miles from home,
we scavenged empty beaches, where waves
had pounded rock smooth. On water
sunlight winked signals we couldn't read.
We surveyed tide pools, our footing
wobbly on mossy rocks. We were left
with what wouldn't wash off, shells
going off in our heads. In that darkness,
you couldn't hurdle bamboo thickets,
tigers feeding on flesh.
A knock at the door granted you retreat
from the swamp we almost crossed.
Streetlight ringing her Medusa hair,
she whispered, *how much longer?*
Fire in the hole, I wound the sheet tighter.
You slipped into starlight,
the door's lock clicking behind you.

4

But the falling of the leaves is not difficult to bear, since they grow again....

—Seneca

WHEN THE POLLEN COUNT IS HIGH

Redbuds uncurl moist leaves.
Each morning tulips open variegated cups.
The grape hyacinths ooze dewy nectar.
Everywhere it is color and fragrance,
lures for whatever will taxi pollen.
Wasps and moths trade this
ménage à trois of reproduction
for sugary beads of perfume.
In the air invisible acrobats
tumble wherever wind whirls them,
little dots winging through air,
launching and lodging,
settling in rock crevices, nasal passages,
the lucky ones snuggling
the black pistils
flaunting their curved stigmas.
The rest of us rub and itch, fill tissues
with sneezes. Meanwhile,
among this flying and floating,
the crabgrass is sending out feelers,
rooting new feet on solid ground,
new anchors ready for their takeover of the yard.

AWAKENING

The attic fan muffled the sound inside
as his hands pushed the screen and lifted.
Dodging lamp, he climbed through the soggy dark.
She woke when he touched her back.
As he covered her mouth, she twisted under the sheet.
He leaned beside her, stared for a long time.

Moonlight lit his silhouette, once her eyes had time
to adjust, once she swallowed her scream inside.
She recognized the dropout who passed her sheets
of notes she never read, never lifted
from her desk. After football games, he leaned back,
cross-armed, against his car when she passed in the dark.

He gathered her from the pillow, smoothed her dark
hair behind her shoulder. She remembered the time
he waited near her locker. His hands trembled on her back
when he pulled her close, laid his forehead inside
the shoulder of her gown. Then he lifted
a hand to brush a breast behind the sheet.

When he lowered his mouth to hers, the sheet
fell away. She felt his wet lips in the dark.
He traced the curve of her cheekbones, then lifted
her face into the thread of moonlight. This time,
he dipped his forehead down to the inside
of her neck, whispering, "Please, just once, kiss me back."

When he found her lips again, she kissed him back.
He squeezed her shoulder before lowering her on the sheet.
Something she didn't understand throbbed inside.

He lay beside her in the moonlit dark,
said, "I've wanted to touch you so many times."
As he inhaled her fragrance, something in her lifted.

He scooped her up once more and lifted
her silky top to touch skin on skin, to lean back
and drink the moment. "This is the only time.
I won't bother you again." He tucked the sheet
around her, turned back into the dark,
leaving her to wonder how he ever got inside.

After she tightened the sheet, heard the screen lift,
he climbed back out the window into the dark.
She lay awake a long time, a moist ache hanging on inside.

SOFTENING UP

With wolves it's easier;
they know where to mark,
how much space they need.
We find limits by stepping outside lines,
walking into plate glass.
In the kitchen you butter gulf shrimp,
set it on the grill to smoke.
While we chew ice cubes, my suitcase
still lingers near the door.
You assure me I'll like the shrimp,
and I do, eating and eating
to keep the taste in my mouth.
While you sort mail,
I hang clothes in the spare room,
both of us waiting for Häagen-Dazs
to soften enough for our spoons.

TWELVE DAYS ON METHADONE

*She may hallucinate but will feel
no pain from the cancer.*
　　　　　　　　—Dr. Davidnor

1

A devil flowed from the switch plate
and imitated me pulling my pain.
Then he stuck a gun to his head.

2

Doctors took tests
while I watched from the ceiling.
They kept filling a basket.
Now what was in the basket?
Not a tisket, a tasket.
It was me.

3

I had a big lunch today,
June peas, the best trout,
and five nectarines.
Your father says I only ate grapes,
but he's wrong.
I ate two nectarines
and gave him two.

4

The doctor said my blood is bad,
but I told him we grew up listening
to that. Doctors should be impartial.
Don't step on that kitten.

5

Have you seen all the little people
in this house? They carved initials
in lampshades. I've been watching
them. They live in the couch pillows.
Sit still; one wearing sunglasses
wants on your lap.

6

Paul Kidwell rode through our yard
yesterday like the Lone Ranger.
He probably ruined your father's grass.
I never knew he had a horse.

7

I told your father I wouldn't go
back to the bedroom until the naked couple
came out from under the bed.
It's amazing what happens
when you're gone for a few days.

8

I can't believe you haven't said *hello*
to your Aunt Mary sitting beside you.
She brought me ice cream.
I told her you and your father
were trying to starve me to death.

9

Last night there was a wall
like in China around the bed.
I knocked on your father's head
until someone answered.
Then he tore it down.

10
Forty people had a party here last night.
They have some illegal ring going.
They offered me ten thousand to keep quiet.
I had to call a lawyer.
Did you know Aunt Lena has a law degree?
Your father tried to stop me
from calling the police, but I got
them here, and they wrote it all down.

11
I couldn't sleep all night.
Those elves across the street
are making puppets for Christmas
on the Kidwells' roof. It's a good thing
kids don't know how foul they talk.

12
I can't understand why your father
lets these animals roam the house.
I couldn't get to the bedroom
until your father moved the cow.
You're looking at me like that again.
Don't start in telling me what's really
happening. I know what I see.

SORTING THINGS OUT

Drawers pulled, a trash bag beside us,
my brother hands me medicine bottles,
canceled checks, instructions
for an abandoned clock. We've worked
our way to his old bedroom, once
off-limits where he hoarded condoms
I found, pirate books he traded for silence.
The mystery of where he went lingered
in shirts he hung on doorknobs.
After he moved out, I knew my brother
through family dinners and card games,
conversations suitable for a table of faces.
Now we sort through Father's estate
as we have most Saturdays, the two of us
unraveling new mysteries: old coins,
unlabeled seeds, birthday cards from widows,
a clove and a toothpick in every jacket pocket.
Today we are sock footed, recalling crowds
he drew when he tangoed at weddings,
the time I wouldn't move off the driveway,
so he pedaled over the teacup in my hand.
After discovering the Mic-O-Say bag,
he sings me camp songs, tells me
the meaning of their Indian names.
We try on Father's hats, tip them back
with old hangers, side step, shoulder to shoulder,
before we lug trash bags to the next room.

GARDENIAS

I can't remember when mistletoe
and males in the same room
stopped making me forget what I was saying,
or when gin tonics between dances
were worth Sunday's hangover.
But gardenias are still arresting
when I enter a room and their scent
hovers near some arrangement.
Like a call from home, they return me
to gardenias my mother grew
and floated in snifters throughout the house.
When she clipped blossoms for our hair,
their ivory faces startling in her chestnut darkness,
the fragrance called us inward,
two women in brown study
returning to their secrets,
forgetting what they were saying,
their eyelashes sometimes aflutter.

BETWEEN TRUTH AND WISH

> *Superstitions lead a kind of half-life in a*
> *twilight world . . . we partly suspend our disbelief*
> *and act as if magic worked.*
> —Margaret Mead

My niece drags Mr. Bunny around the yard
in pursuit of our dogs. My neighbor says
her son hung on to a blanket she could
only wash while he was sleeping.
Years later, when he had his own child,
she presented her son with the silky scrap
wrapped in plastic. I tell her about a day
my mother and I cleaned the attic.
We rummaged through Christmas bulbs,
bent cookie tins, stuffed animals I'd collected.
We tossed turtle, fox, panda. *Bed ornaments,*
mother said, *except the black dog you carried*
everywhere. I lifted the shapeless mound,
its limp head drooping over a fuzzless shoulder.
I took it to put in my cedar chest
with the wool muff I don't remember.
Across the yard Reyna is serving tea
and rock cookies to Mr. Bunny and the dogs,
lying beside her on a beach towel.
She scolds Mr. Bunny for taking three cookies.
My neighbor and I return to our gardens.
I weed around parsley, scatter a seed head
in the bare spots for the next crop.
Unhooking a caterpillar clinging to a peppery curl,
I remember wearing my mother's Pendleton jacket
for two weeks after she died. Father's cuff links
I slipped inside a medicine-bag necklace,
half-lives I needed between truth and wish.

I gather up pruners, basket of basil and bergamot,
ready to take us in for peaches and cinnamon toast.
Reyna and the dogs have fallen asleep,
her head on Zinnia, her feet across Zeke,
Mr. Bunny tucked under an arm.

HOMING

The ants are scaling the bathroom hamper again,
sliding around in the sink. Every spring
when heavy rains rush through storm drains,
I find them singlefiling up a table leg, shimmying
under windows. The exterminator tells me
they are confused, lost, getting in from the rain.
I remind him they come back every year.
He drizzles Dursban along moldings, soaks
the doorway carpet, says they prefer the outdoors.
I follow him from room to room, ask how I
can stop them from dropping down rafters
onto stored photo albums and paint cans
like paratroopers on a mission.
The exterminator hands me my bill,
already thinking about his next customer.
My neighbor shakes his head, removes his cap
to scratch his forehead. No ants have marched
under his doors. Like my doctor, the exterminator
is good with symptoms. In a day or two I find
strays tucked into black dots. This year I'll insulate,
plant tansy around the foundation, sprinkle granules
when I smell rain. I want the little Oedipuses
to stop coming home.

LATE AUGUST

For Sonya

My friend's family welcomed us in,
two beacons carrying bags of articles,
tapes for pain imaging, but no magic
tincture, no herb to erase damage. A sign
above the fireplace said, "Bob's Team,"
and eight penetrating faces wore matching
t-shirts with photos of Bob. On the floor
sat a diapered grandson in his own t-shirt:
"I'm Little Bob." We talked about vitamins,
diet, people who will themselves well.
Bob crossed his arms and shook his head.
We moved him to a straight-backed chair,
formed a circle around him. Only his
lungs wrestling with breath punctuated
the voice of Margery's meditation.
In this circle of hands was a presence
as real as a quiet moment when sunlight
slants through shocks of new leaves.
I wanted my friend's father to breathe
easy again. I wanted my friend to feel
light and weightless as kites lifting above trees.
But this was August before the last autumn.
Already yellowed leaves were letting go, spinning
downward, their arms folded in.
I found on their driveway a dead cicada,
patches of its wing shredded in the center.
Its iridescence flickered in the fading sunlight.
A mottled leaf twisted in its short journey
to the driveway near the cicada, where
it swerved and bumped along before it stopped.

CHILLY IN OUR GOWNS

My doctor used to clip articles from our town paper.
My fencing victory and engagement photo grinned
when he opened my chart. We compared tomato
yields, recommended books. He listened
to my lungs, my heart, examined my throat,
but always the laying on of hands, the patted
shoulder before a shot, the outstretched
arm rescuing me from the hypoglycemic faint
to offer a hamburger and a malt. I could name
states he'd toured with his daughters, night classes
he took on the Middle East. Now,
his nurse takes my blood pressure and asks
if I think it will rain. She writes symptoms
on my chart. My doctor no longer sits,
one arm resting on his knee, to ask
if I'm still taking calcium, drinking water.
He looks out the window, a quick brown study
he doesn't share. He is behind, his waiting room
sinking under sore throats, a broken toe,
a stitchable biking accident. He writes
prescriptions, orders tests, has technicians
do his touching. He rushes off to others,
waiting chilly in their gowns. I scuttle out one door
as he closes another, his muffled voice
an instant replay. The receptionist assures me
the nurse will call, my doctor no longer
my ferryman across fear's murky water.

TO THE BONE

For Randy Bates
1954–1987

We carry yellow roses, pecan clusters,
a silver balloon. Down long hallways,
voices bounce and break as we
concentrate on room numbers.
In a waiting room, someone knits
a sweater, a family considers
Aunt Bea's options. Each visit
is a loved one's heart attack
or surgery all over: the beep
of monitors, bagged silver poles,
stiff neck, tea in the coffee shop,
the turning of magazine pages.
I imagined your room, though miles away,
was like others, cup of ice, pitcher
on bed tray, television hinged to wall,
but nurses tightened their gloves
when drawing your blood; everything
you touched they tossed into the disposal
marked with an X. You told me *no*
to coming, told me to remember
salmon dinners cozy with wine,
shopping for perfume at Sak's,
olives at Scimeca's. Your voice
unraveled across the line, misstrung
sentences I rearranged. You were
an abbreviation retelling the time
you and Ann joked after the reunion,
and the night we read old yearbooks,
howling at what others predicted
you'd do with your life. I was left

to imagine you a Goya child,
the tinker toy bone of an arm draped
over an unfinished crossword. I've seen
hollowed eye sockets, skin loose on the bone.
No, you said. *No.* Then your sister's voice
saying she'd brought you home. I carried
around that last day: you lifting your
briefcase, trench coat over an arm,
red and yellow leaves falling all around you,
that final hug we never know is the last.

LONG-DISTANCE LOVE

Tonight we need not wait for sleep
to nurse the thousand-mile wave,
the six-week kiss we carried
from train station or airport
like forbidden stash.
Tonight the hot voice of want talks us down:
we fumble with buttons, unzip our passion,
climb out of trappings
for the silky marriage of skin.
Under the sofa quilt we tunnel
into kisses and fingers inching their way,
into the buoyant wake of wet places,
into the warm thrust of long-distance love,
the echo of keys still dangling from the lock.

DEPTH FINDER

I can't see my husband from the study,
but I know he's at the window looking out,
thinking as he waters the hibiscus.
He loves the silence of his plants
reaching up, new blooms like offerings.
I know he's watching the wind
dipping and lifting the leaves outside.
He knows about wind and direction,
about feeding his sails so his boat
leans and skims towards the dam.
He says little as he stares across the lake,
as though he's listening to the wind's
breath and his own become one.
He needs only a depth finder so we
don't go aground. This is my job,
to monitor depth. At times, I pull
wench ropes. Tonight, I hear the water
soaking the plants, the wind setting off
the chimes. I join my husband where
he stares out the window. Sometimes
when I stand on the bow as he glides us
into the cove, I can almost touch what he feels.

Maryfrances Wagner's books include *Salvatore's Daughter* (BkMk Press), *Light Subtracts Itself, Red Silk* (Thorpe Menn Book Award for Literary Excellence), *Dioramas, Pouf, The Silence of Red Glass,* and *The Immigrants' New Camera.* Poems have appeared in *New Letters, Midwest Quarterly, Laurel Review, Rattle, River Styx, Main Street Rag, Green Mountains Review, Tar River Review, Voices in Italian Americana, Unsettling America: An Anthology of Contemporary Multicultural Poetry* (Penguin Books), *Literature Across Cultures* (Pearson/Longman), *Bearing Witness, The Dream Book, An Anthology of Writings by Italian American Women* (American Book Award from the Before Columbus Foundation), etc. She co-edits *I-70 Review* and served as individual artist honoree for the Missouri Arts Awards, the state's highest honor in the arts. She is now serving as Missouri's poet laureate for 2021-2023. For more information, check her website: http://maryfranceswagnerwriter.fieldinfoserv.com/

BkMk Press began celebrating its fiftieth anniversary in 2021. After thirty-eight years at the University of Missouri-Kansas City, BkMk returned to being an independent press in 2021. BkMk Press is grateful for the support it has received in recent years from the following organizations and individuals:

Missouri Arts Council
Miller-Mellor Foundation
Neptune Foundation
Richard J. Stern Foundation for the Arts
Stanley H. Durwood Foundation
William T. Kemper Foundation
Anonymous
Dwight Arn
Beverly Burch
Jaimee Wriston Colbert
Maija Rhee Devine
Ben Furnish
Charles Egan
Alice Friman
Anna Jaffe
Michael Jaffe
Tamar Jaffe and Mike Reyes Whitney and Mariella Kerr
Carla Klausner
Lorraine M. López
Patricia Cleary Miller
Margot Patterson
Peppermint Creek Theatre Company
Elizabeth Goldring Piene
Alan Proctor
James Hugo Rifenbark
Sylvia Stuckey
Roderick and Wyatt Townley